GRAPHIC BIOGRAPHIES

Christopher COLUMBUS

famous explorer

by Mary Dodson Wade

illustrated by

Rod Whigham and Charles Barnett III

Consultant:

Keith A. Pickering, Associate Editor

Dio: The International Journal of Scientific History

Capstone press®

Mankato, Minnesota

Graphic Library is published by Capstone Press,
151 Good Counsel Drive, P.O. Box 669, Mankato, Minnesota 56002.
www.capstonepress.com

Printed in the United States of America

1 2 3 4 5 6 12 11 10 09 08 07

Library of Congress Cataloging-in-Publication Data
Wade, Mary Dodson.
Christopher Columbus : famous explorer / by Mary Dodson Wade; illustrated by Rod Whigham and Charles Barnett III.
p. cm.—(Graphic library. Graphic biographies)
Summary: "In graphic novel format, tells the life story of Christopher Columbus and his discovery of the Americas"—Provided by publisher.
Includes bibliographical references and index.
Audience: Grades 4–6.
ISBN–13: 978-0-7368-6853-2 (hardcover)
ISBN–10: 0-7368-6853-4 (hardcover)
ISBN–13: 978-0-7368-7905-7 (softcover pbk.)
ISBN–10: 0-7368-7905-6 (softcover pbk.)
1. Columbus, Christopher—Juvenile literature. 2. Explorers—America—Biography—Juvenile literature. 3. Explorers—Spain—Biography—Juvenile literature. 4. America—Discovery and exploration—Spanish—Juvenile literature. 5. Graphic novels. I. Whigham, Rod, 1954– II. Barnett, Charles, III. III. Title. IV. Series.
E111.W244 2007
970.01'5092—dc22 2006023793

Designers
Bob Lentz and Kyle Grenz

Colorist
Melissa Kaercher

Editor
Aaron Sautter

Editor's note: Direct quotations from primary sources are indicated by a yellow background.

Direct quotations appear on the following pages:
Pages 10, 11, 18, from *The Worlds of Christopher Columbus* by William D. Phillips, Jr. and Carla Rahn Phillips (New York: Cambridge University Press, 1992).
Page 21, from *The Life of the Admiral Christopher Columbus by His Son Ferdinand* by Fernando Colón, Translated by Benjamin Keen (New Brunswick, N.J.: Rutgers University Press, 1992).

Table of Contents

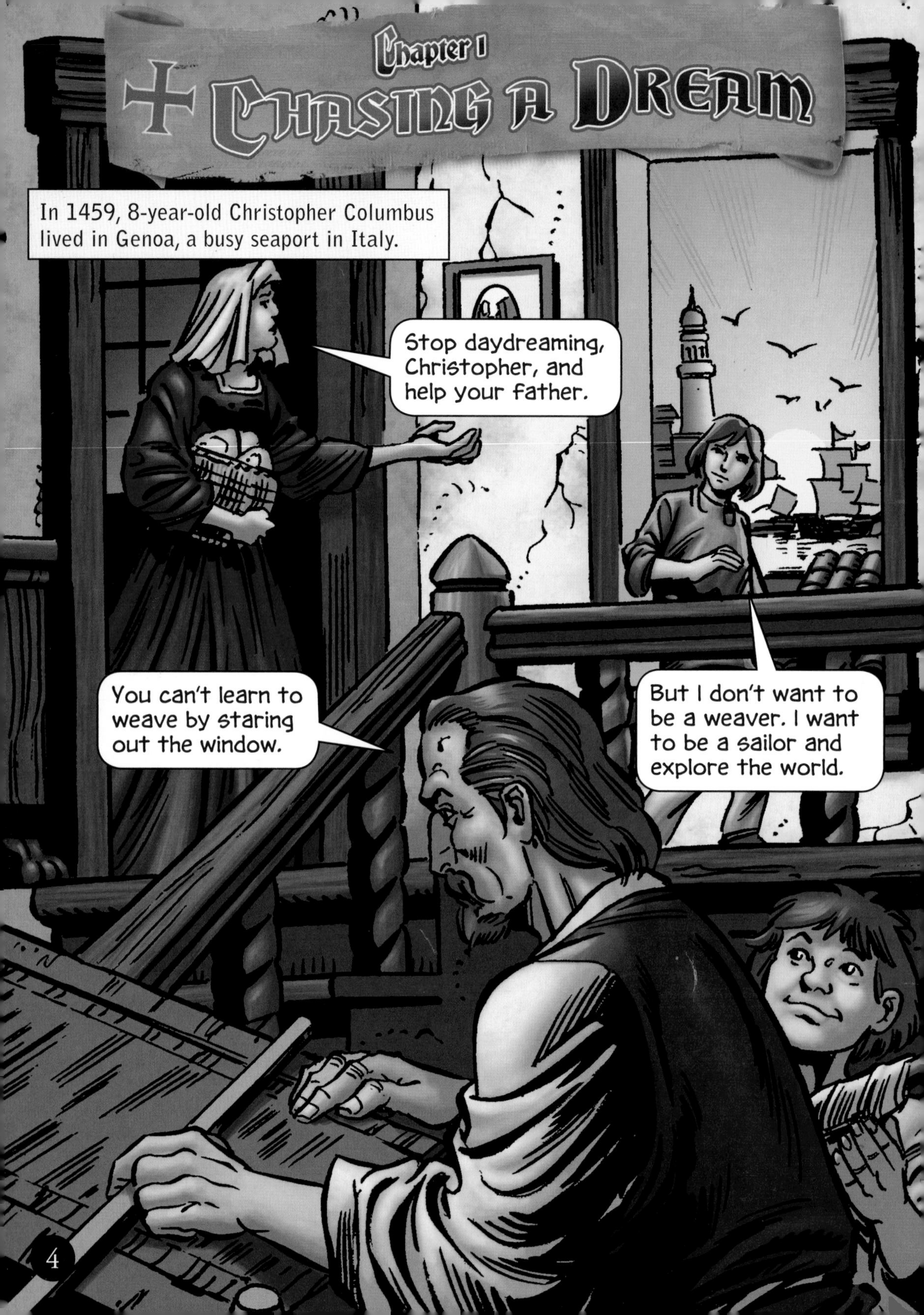
Chapter 1
Chasing a Dream
In 1459, 8-year-old Christopher Columbus lived in Genoa, a busy seaport in Italy.
Stop daydreaming, Christopher, and help your father.
You can't learn to weave by staring out the window.
But I don't want to be a weaver. I want to be a sailor and explore the world.

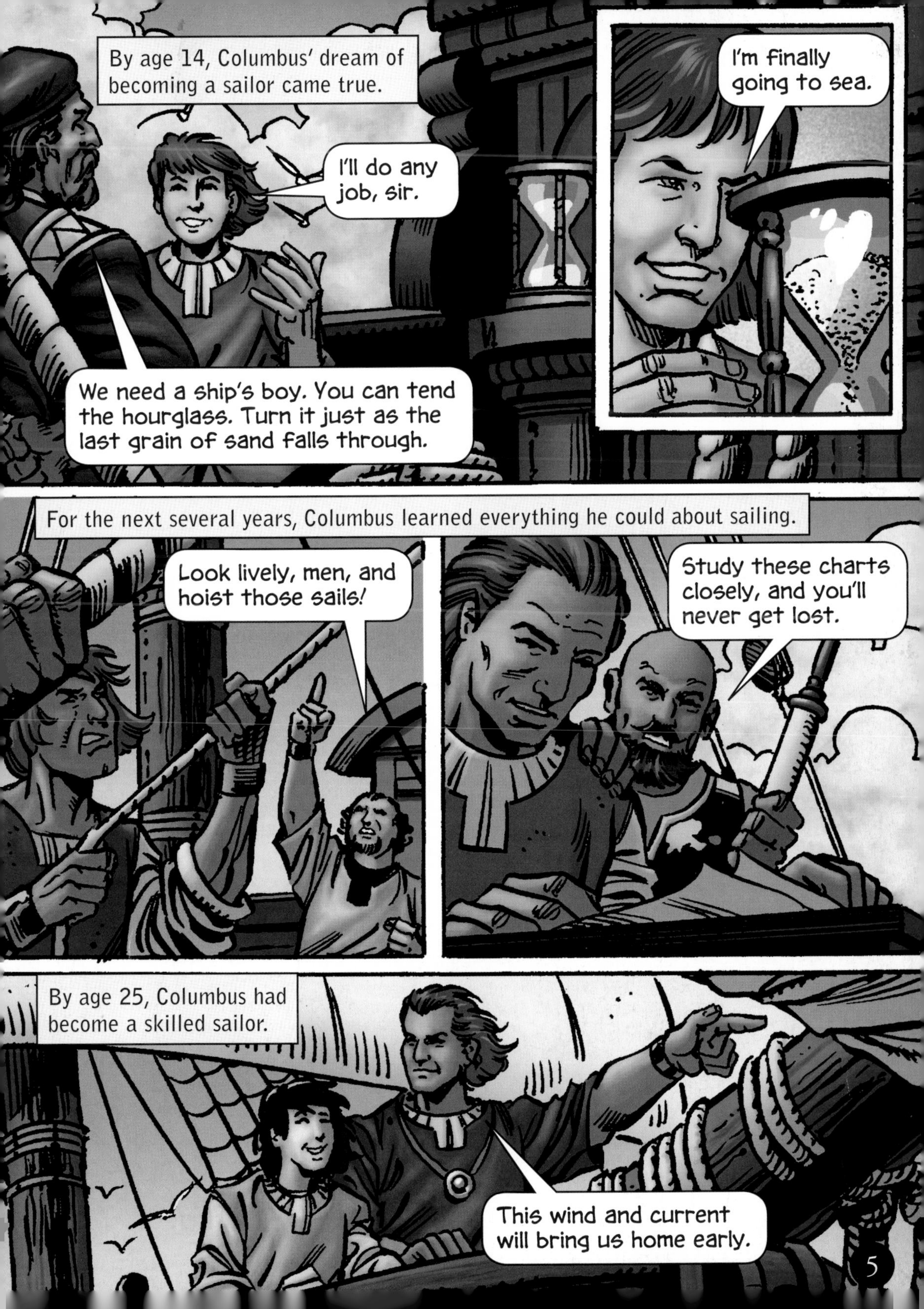
By age 14, Columbus' dream of becoming a sailor came true.
I'll do any job, sir.
We need a ship's boy. You can tend the hourglass. Turn it just as the last grain of sand falls through.
I'm finally going to sea.
For the next several years, Columbus learned everything he could about sailing.
Look lively, men, and hoist those sails!
Study these charts closely, and you'll never get lost.
By age 25, Columbus had become a skilled sailor.
This wind and current will bring us home early.

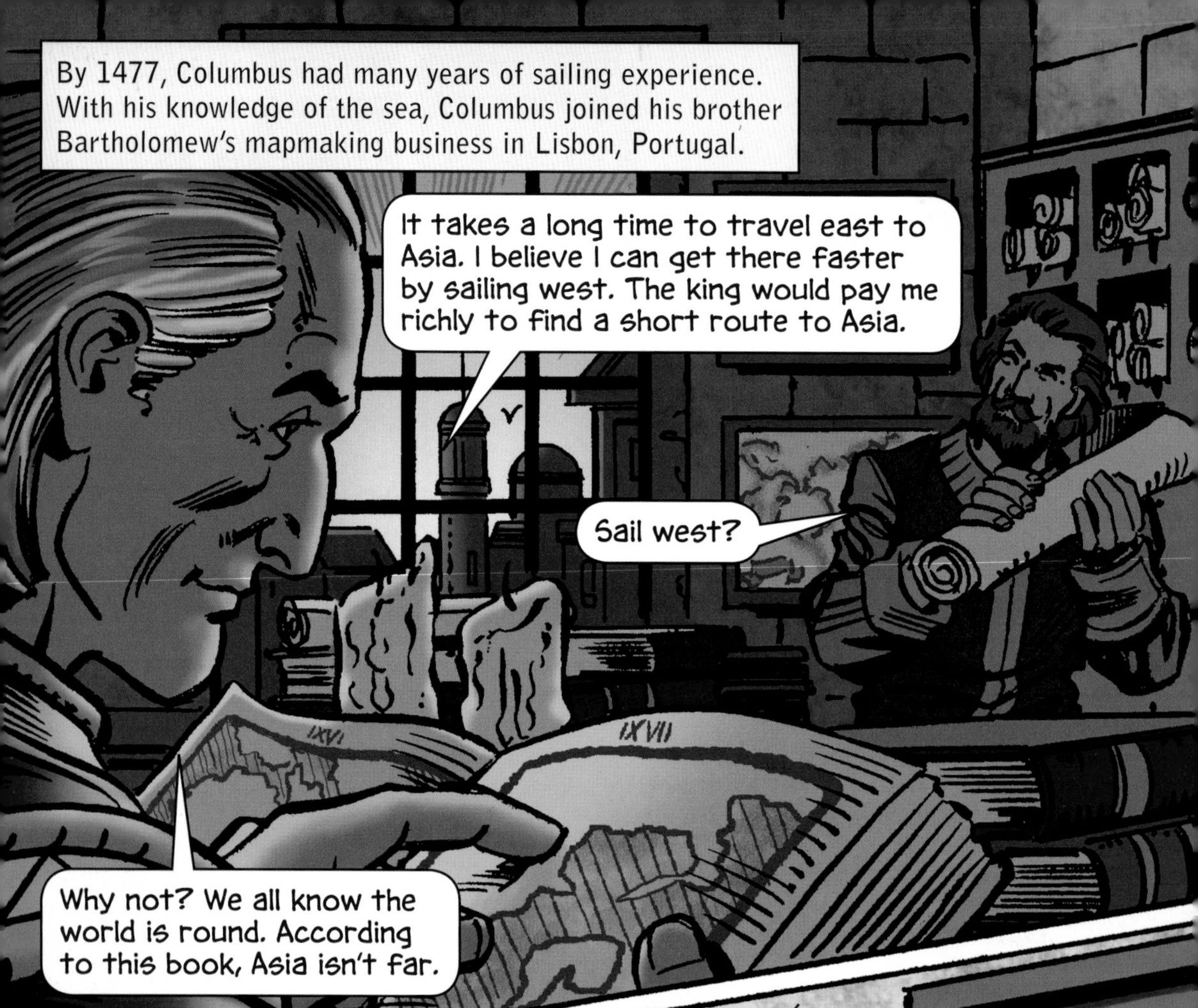
By 1477, Columbus had many years of sailing experience. With his knowledge of the sea, Columbus joined his brother Bartholomew's mapmaking business in Lisbon, Portugal.
It takes a long time to travel east to Asia. I believe I can get there faster by sailing west. The king would pay me richly to find a short route to Asia.
Sail west?
Why not? We all know the world is round. According to this book, Asia isn't far.

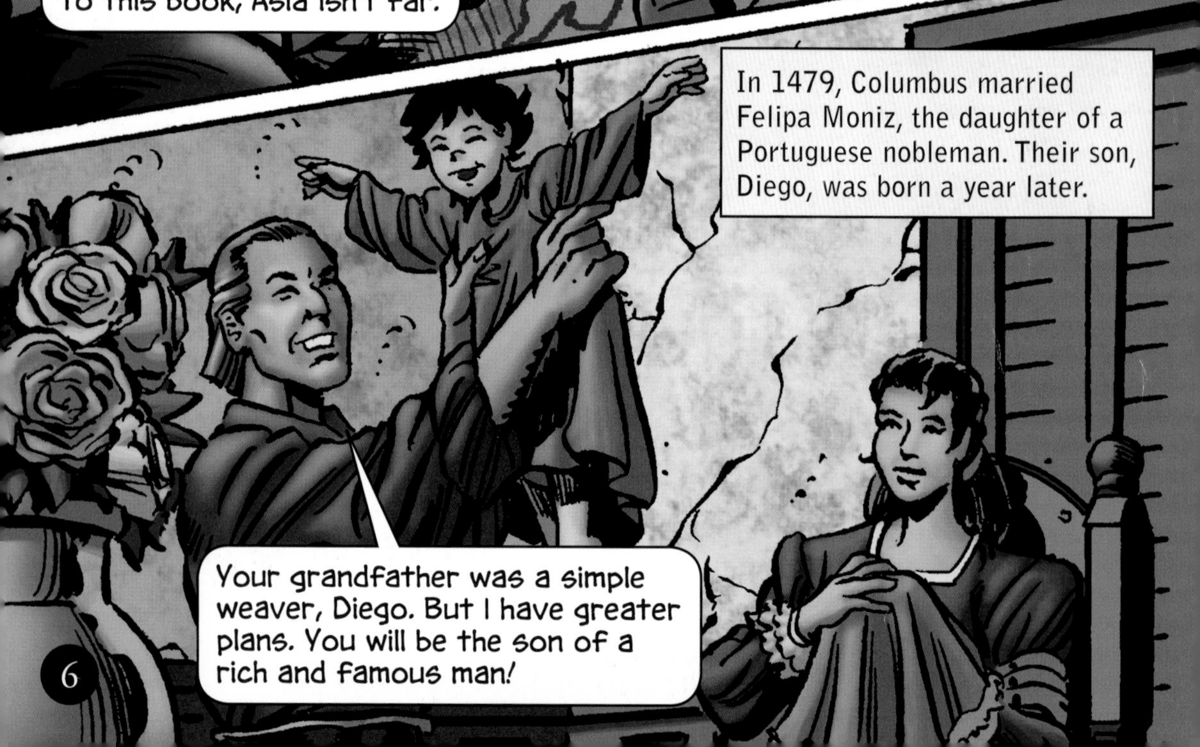
In 1479, Columbus married Felipa Moniz, the daughter of a Portuguese nobleman. Their son, Diego, was born a year later.
Your grandfather was a simple weaver, Diego. But I have greater plans. You will be the son of a rich and famous man!

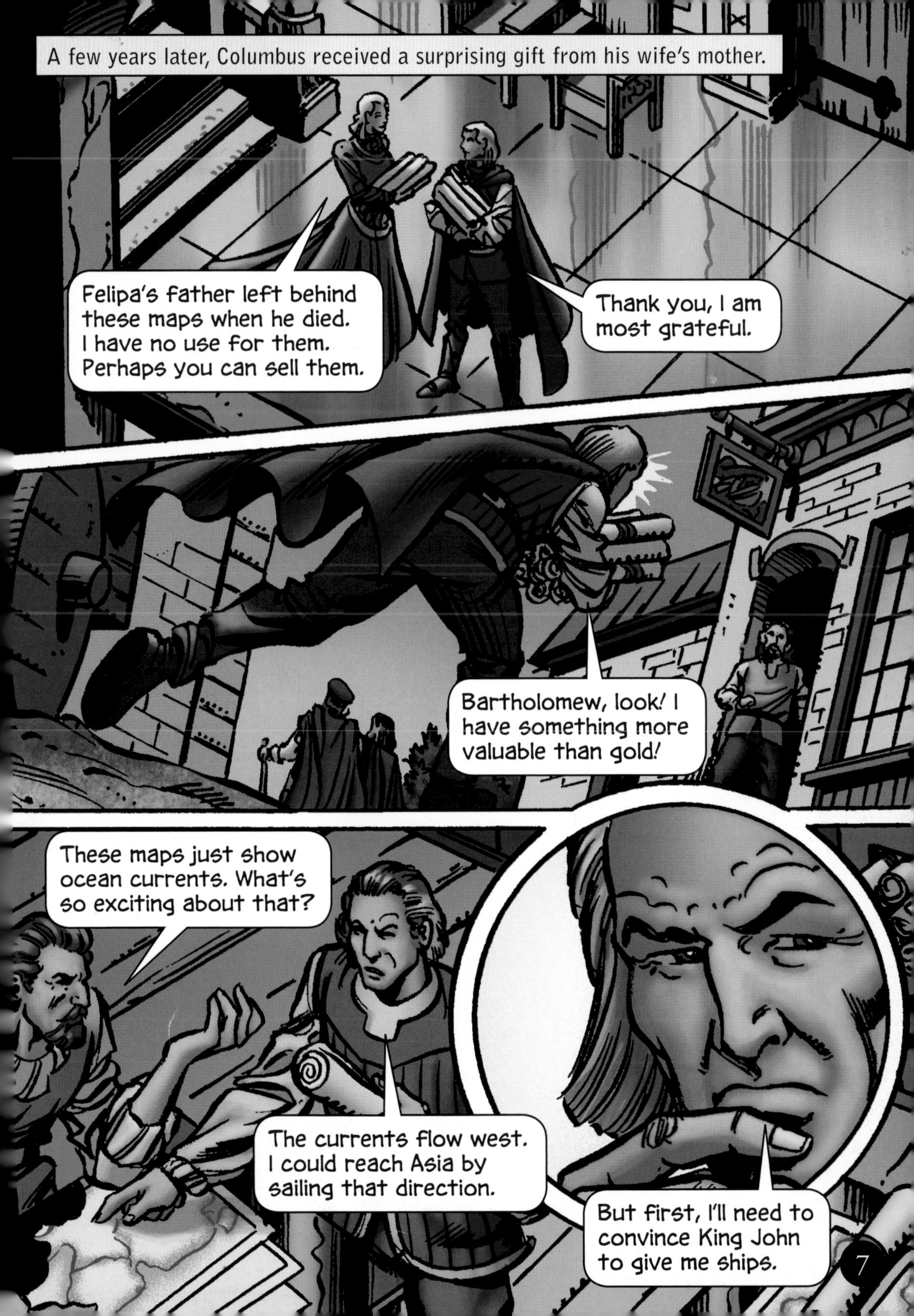
A few years later, Columbus received a surprising gift from his wife's mother.
Felipa's father left behind these maps when he died. I have no use for them. Perhaps you can sell them.
Thank you, I am most grateful.
Bartholomew, look! I have something more valuable than gold!
These maps just show ocean currents. What's so exciting about that?
The currents flow west. I could reach Asia by sailing that direction.
But first, I'll need to convince King John to give me ships.

Chapter 2
A Dream Come True

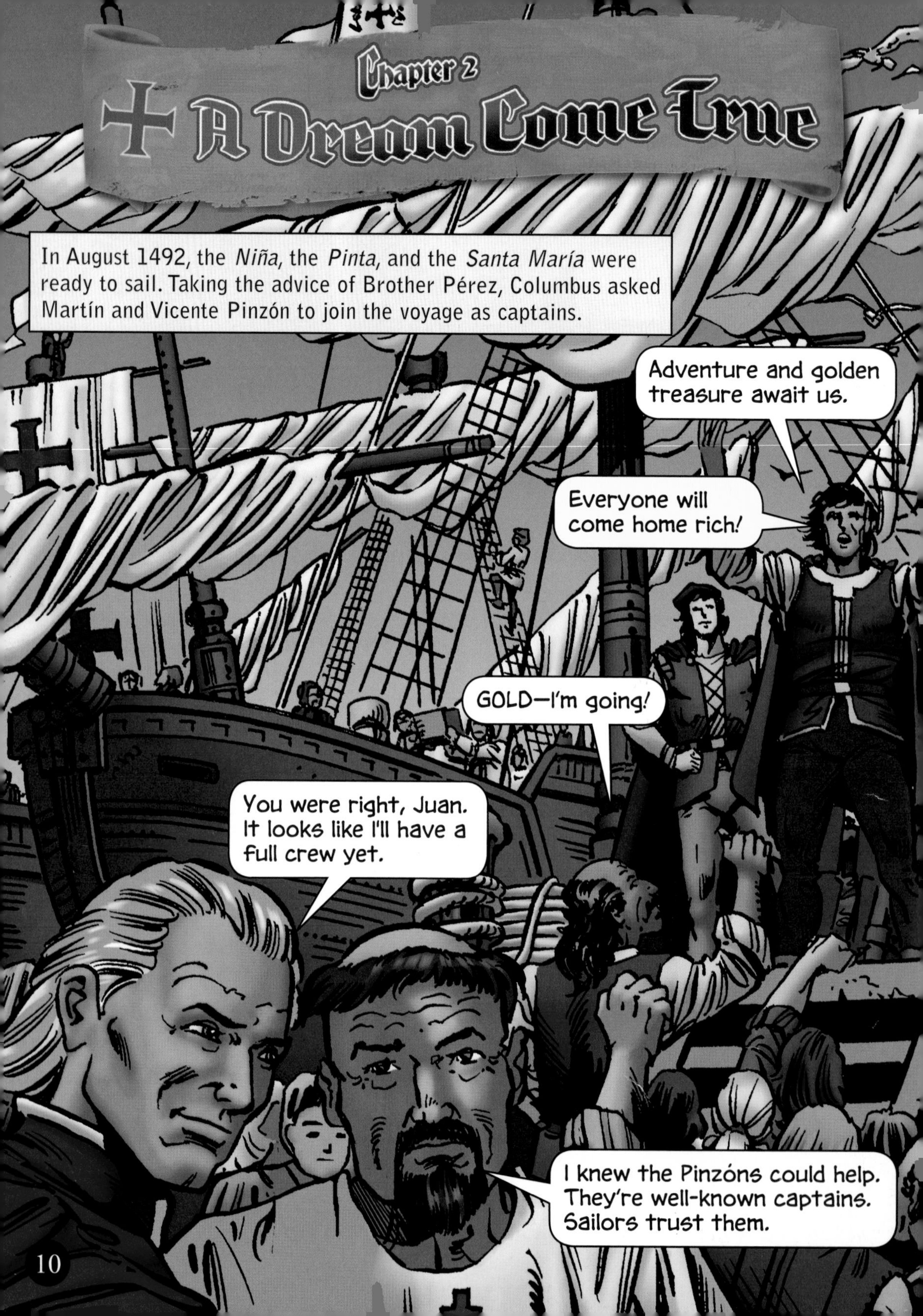

In August 1492, the *Niña*, the *Pinta*, and the *Santa María* were ready to sail. Taking the advice of Brother Pérez, Columbus asked Martín and Vicente Pinzón to join the voyage as captains.
Adventure and golden treasure await us.
Everyone will come home rich!
GOLD—I'm going!
You were right, Juan. It looks like I'll have a full crew yet.
I knew the Pinzóns could help. They're well-known captains. Sailors trust them.

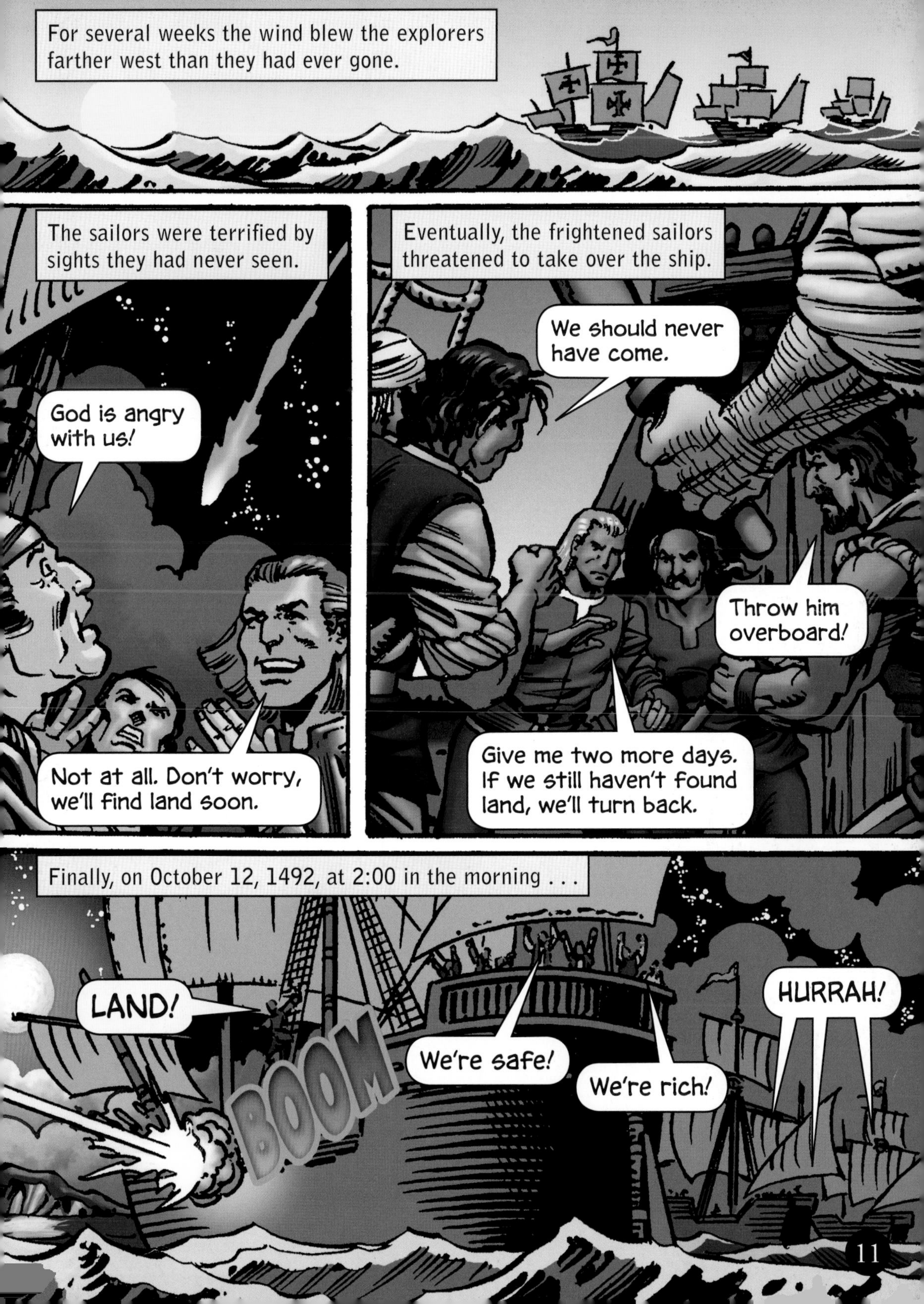
For several weeks the wind blew the explorers farther west than they had ever gone.
The sailors were terrified by sights they had never seen.
God is angry with us!
Not at all. Don't worry, we'll find land soon.
Eventually, the frightened sailors threatened to take over the ship.
We should never have come.
Throw him overboard!
Give me two more days. If we still haven't found land, we'll turn back.
Finally, on October 12, 1492, at 2:00 in the morning . . .
LAND!
BOOM
We're safe!
We're rich!
HURRAH!

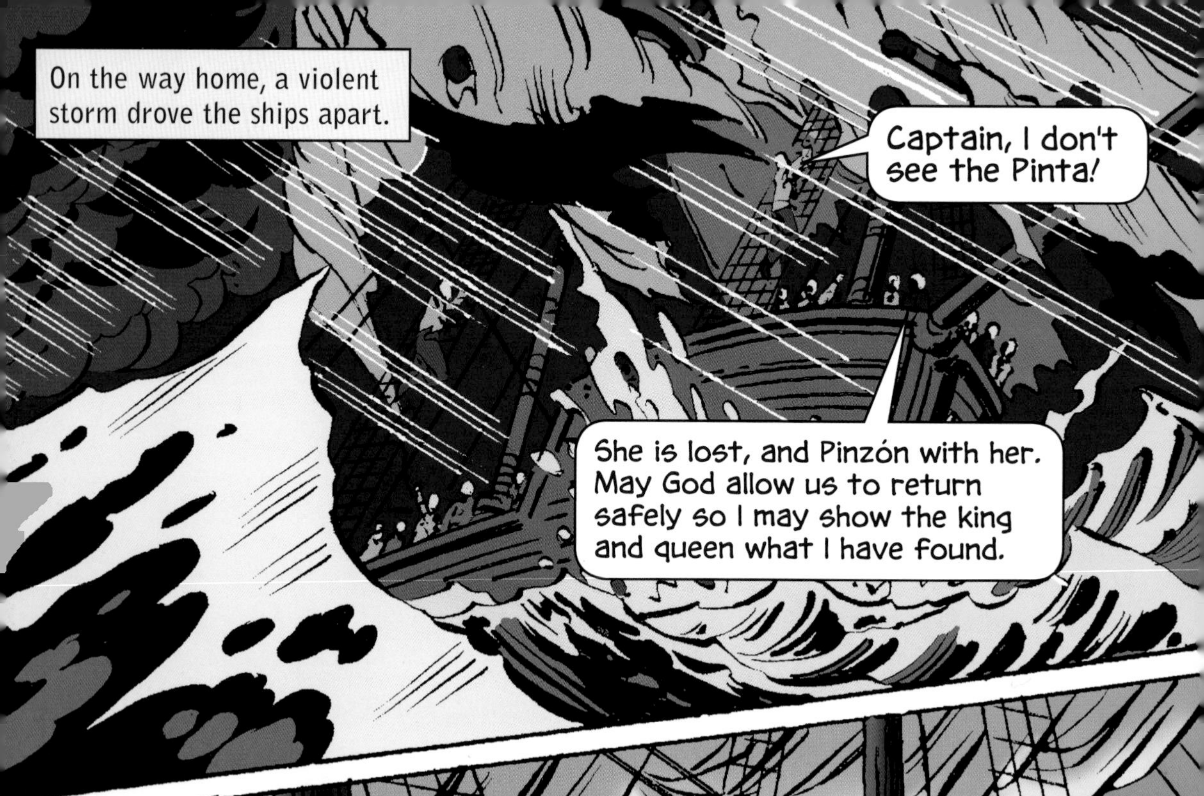
On the way home, a violent storm drove the ships apart.
Captain, I don't see the Pinta!
She is lost, and Pinzón with her. May God allow us to return safely so I may show the king and queen what I have found.

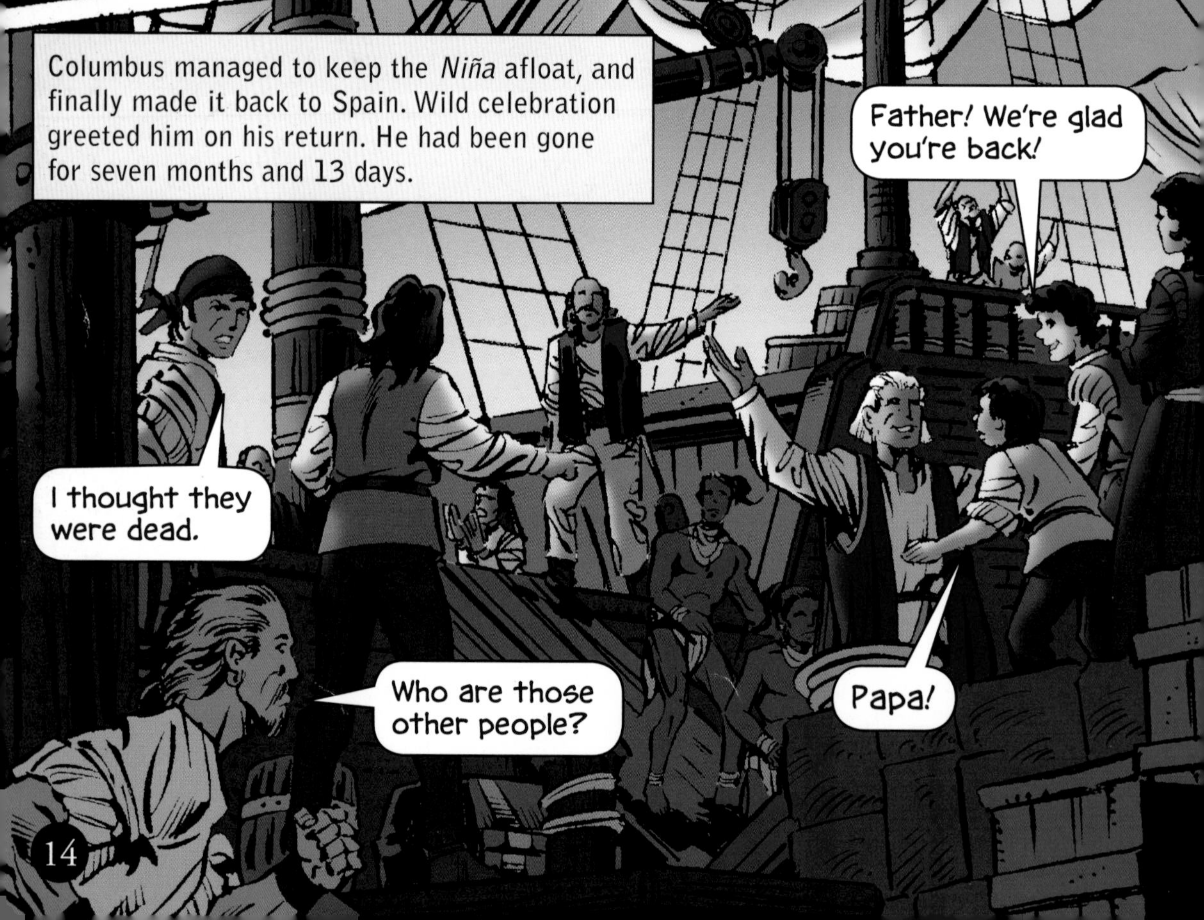
Columbus managed to keep the *Niña* afloat, and finally made it back to Spain. Wild celebration greeted him on his return. He had been gone for seven months and 13 days.
Father! We're glad you're back!
I thought they were dead.
Who are those other people?
Papa!

15

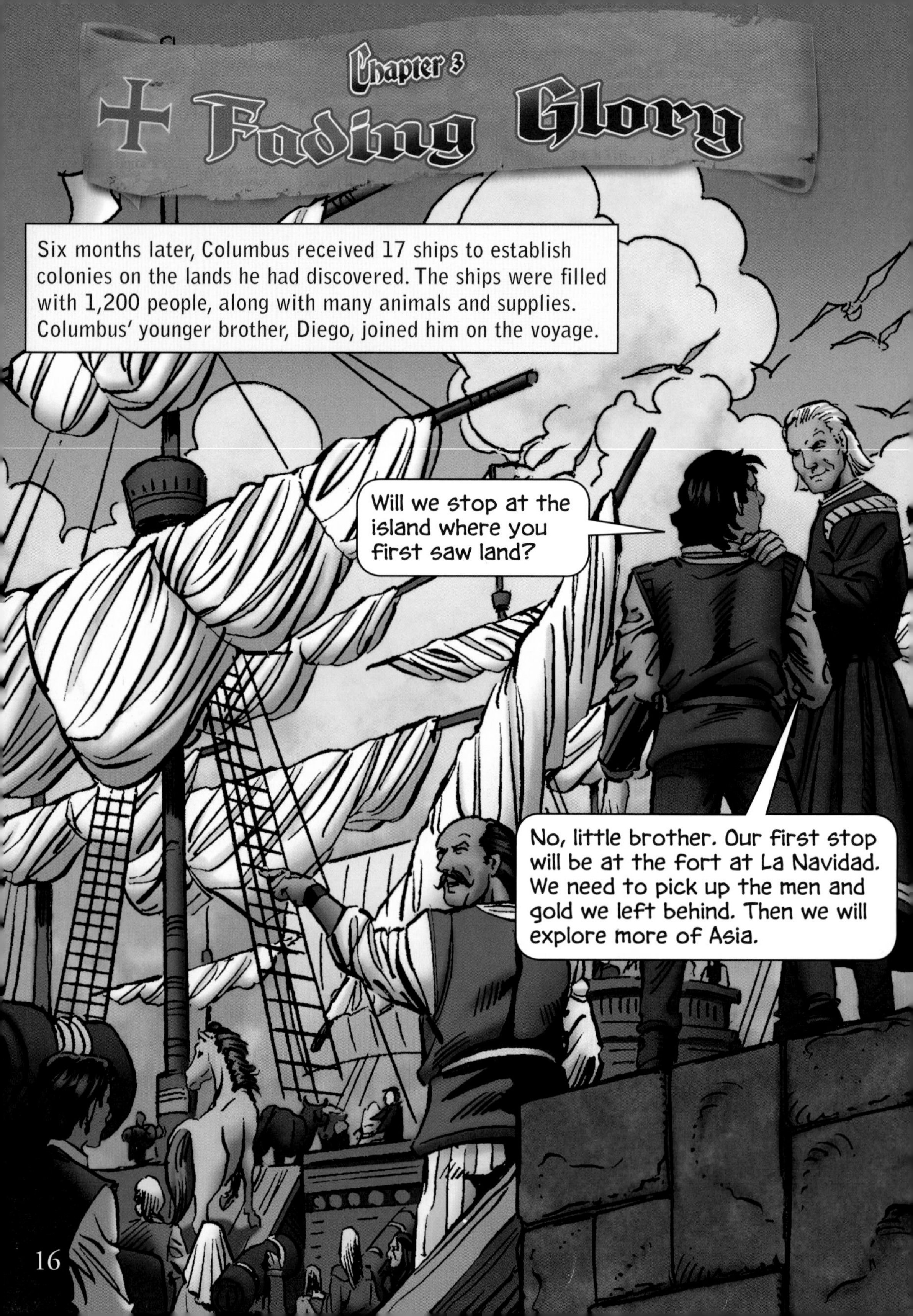
Chapter 3
Fading Glory
Six months later, Columbus received 17 ships to establish colonies on the lands he had discovered. The ships were filled with 1,200 people, along with many animals and supplies. Columbus' younger brother, Diego, joined him on the voyage.
Will we stop at the island where you first saw land?
No, little brother. Our first stop will be at the fort at La Navidad. We need to pick up the men and gold we left behind. Then we will explore more of Asia.

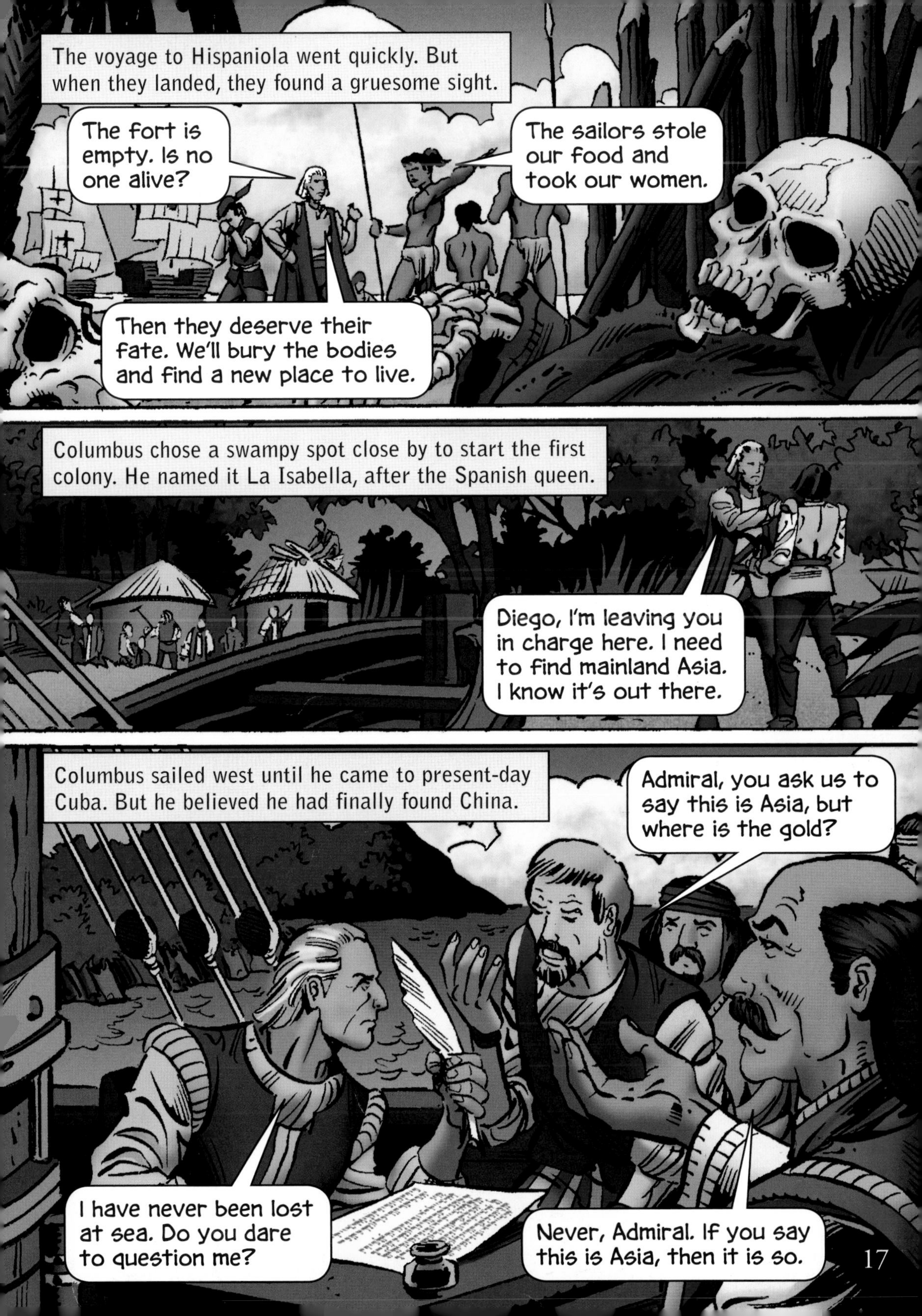
The voyage to Hispaniola went quickly. But when they landed, they found a gruesome sight.
The fort is empty. Is no one alive?
The sailors stole our food and took our women.
Then they deserve their fate. We'll bury the bodies and find a new place to live.
Columbus chose a swampy spot close by to start the first colony. He named it La Isabella, after the Spanish queen.
Diego, I'm leaving you in charge here. I need to find mainland Asia. I know it's out there.
Columbus sailed west until he came to present-day Cuba. But he believed he had finally found China.
Admiral, you ask us to say this is Asia, but where is the gold?
I have never been lost at sea. Do you dare to question me?
Never, Admiral. If you say this is Asia, then it is so.

Many months went by with no sign of rescue. The Indians soon grew tired of bringing food to the marooned sailors. But Columbus knew an eclipse of the moon was coming. He formed a plan to trick the natives into cooperating.

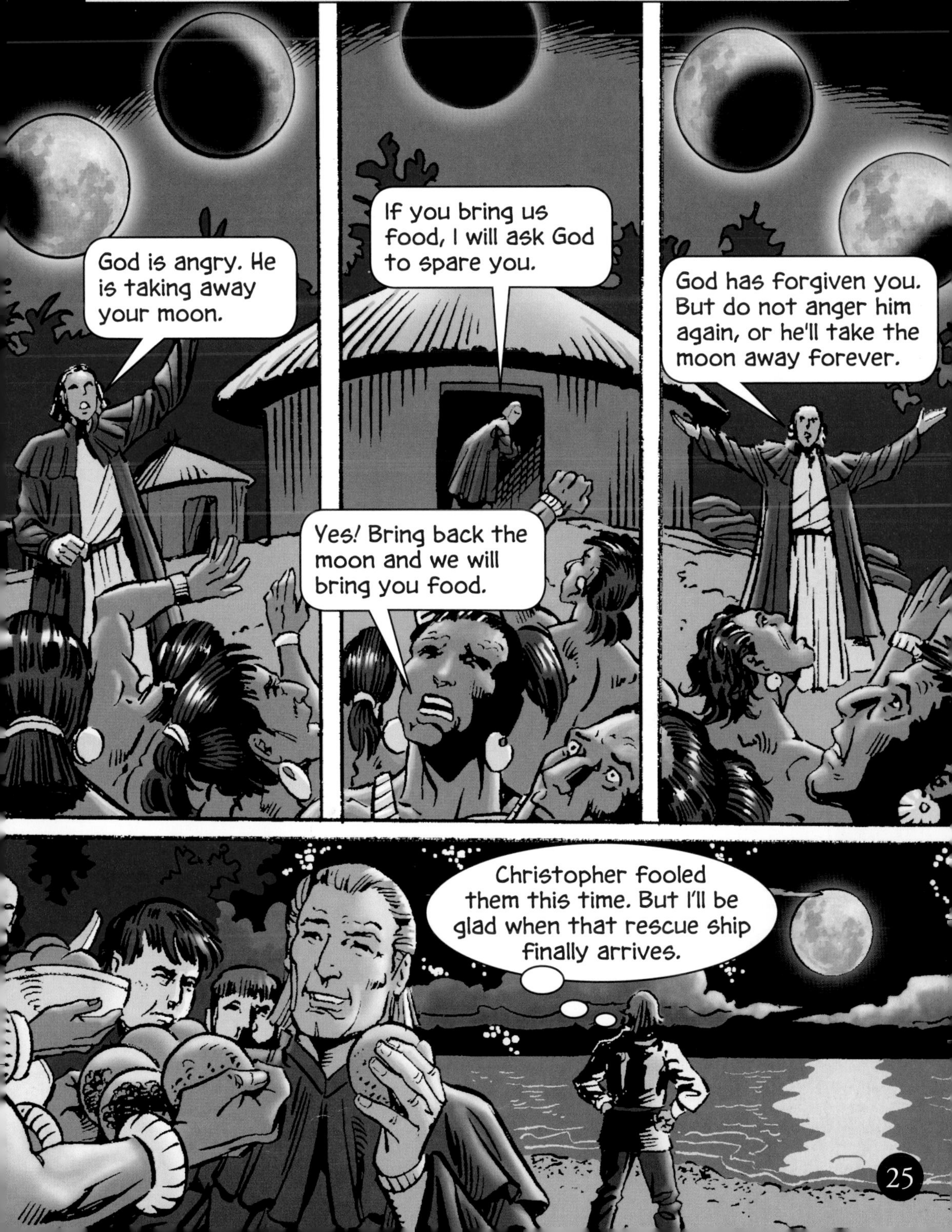
God is angry. He is taking away your moon.
If you bring us food, I will ask God to spare you.
Yes! Bring back the moon and we will bring you food.
God has forgiven you. But do not anger him again, or he'll take the moon away forever.
Christopher fooled them this time. But I'll be glad when that rescue ship finally arrives.

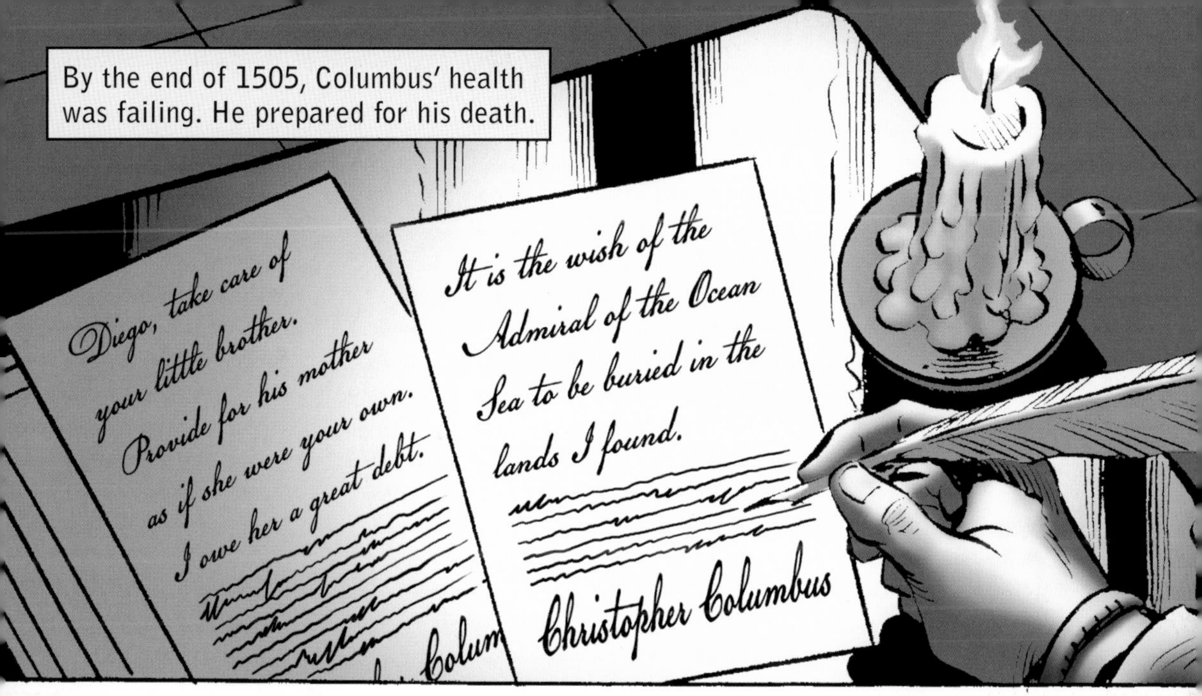
By the end of 1505, Columbus' health was failing. He prepared for his death.
Diego, take care of your little brother. Provide for his mother as if she were your own. I owe her a great debt.
It is the wish of the Admiral of the Ocean Sea to be buried in the lands I found.
Christopher Columbus

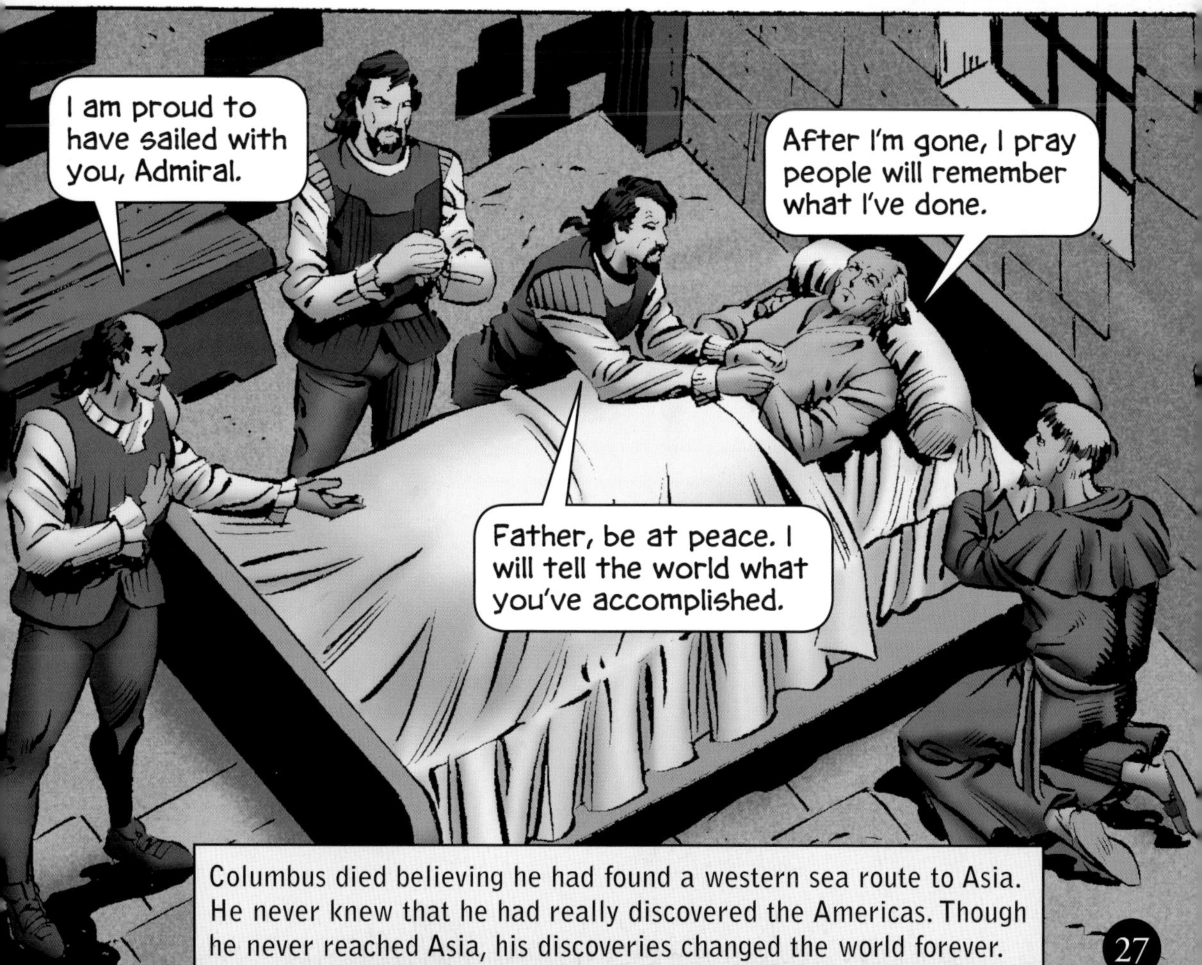
I am proud to have sailed with you, Admiral.
After I'm gone, I pray people will remember what I've done.
Father, be at peace. I will tell the world what you've accomplished.
Columbus died believing he had found a western sea route to Asia. He never knew that he had really discovered the Americas. Though he never reached Asia, his discoveries changed the world forever.

More about
✝ Christopher Columbus

✝ Columbus was born in 1451, in Genoa, Italy. He died on May 20, 1506, in Valladolid, Spain.

✝ Though it was the flagship, the *Santa María* was much slower than the *Niña* and *Pinta*. Columbus preferred the *Niña*. The sturdy little ship made three round-trip voyages across the Atlantic Ocean.

✝ Columbus usually sailed by using "dead reckoning." He used a compass to keep the ship moving in the right direction. He measured the distance traveled by noting how fast a floating object passed by the ship. Dead reckoning allowed him to find his way without using landmarks.

✝ Martín Pinzón didn't die in the storm on the return trip from the first voyage. He arrived at Spain only hours after Columbus did. But he died a few weeks later. Vicente Pinzón returned to explore the coast of South America. The Pinzón family later claimed they had a right to part of the newly discovered lands. Their claims were the basis for years of lawsuits. King Ferdinand used these claims to limit Columbus' rights and certain privileges.

✠ No pictures of Columbus were painted during his life. People who knew him said he was tall with a long nose, red hair, and light-colored eyes. His hair turned completely white by the time he was 30 years old.

✠ Ferdinand Columbus became a well-known scholar and wrote a biography about his father's life and discoveries. He also saved many of the notes written by his father, which still exist today.

✠ Columbus made a fifth voyage after he died. In 1537, his body was sent to Santo Domingo. More than 350 years later, Columbus' remains were returned to Spain. But 20 years later, workers in Santo Domingo found a box of bones with Columbus' name on it. Some people think the bones that were taken to Spain were really those of Christopher's younger brother, Diego, who had been made governor of the colony after Christopher died. In 1992, a new monument was built to house the remains of both men. Today, nobody knows which bones are those of Christopher and which are his brother's.

GLOSSARY

colony (KOL-uh-nee)—an area that is settled and ruled by people from another country

hourglass (OUR-glass)—an instrument for measuring time

monastery (MAH-nuh-ster-ee)—a group of buildings where monks live and work

noble (NOH-buhl)—a wealthy, upper-class person of high rank

Taíno (TYE-no)—the tribe of Indians who met Columbus on San Salvador

trade route (TRADE ROUT)—a road or course set up to allow people to exchange goods

INTERNET SITES

FactHound offers a safe, fun way to find Internet sites related to this book. All of the sites on FactHound have been researched by our staff.

Here's how:
1. Visit *www.facthound.com*
2. Choose your grade level.
3. Type in this book ID **0736868534** for age-appropriate sites. You may also browse subjects by clicking on letters, or by clicking on pictures and words.
4. Click on the **Fetch It** button.

FactHound will fetch the best sites for you!

READ MORE

Aller, Susan Bivin. *Christopher Columbus*. History Maker Bios. Minneapolis: Lerner, 2003.

Doak, Robin S. *Christopher Columbus: Explorer of the New World*. Signature Lives. Minneapolis: Compass Point Books, 2005.

Kaufman, Mervyn D. *Christopher Columbus*. Fact Finders. Biographies. Mankato, Minn.: Capstone Press, 2004.

Molzahn, Arlene B. *Christopher Columbus: Famous Explorer*. Explorers! Berkely Heights, N.J.: Enslow, 2003.

BIBLIOGRAPHY

Colón, Fernando. *The Life of the Admiral Christopher Columbus by His Son Ferdinand.* Translated by Benjamin Keen. New Brunswick, N.J.: Rutgers University Press, 1992.

Landström, Björn. *Columbus: The Story of Don Cristóbal Colón, Admiral of the Ocean, and his Four Voyages Westward to the Indies According to Contemporary Sources.* New York: The Macmillan Company, 1967.

Phillips, William D., and Carla Rahn Phillips. *The Worlds of Christopher Columbus*. New York: Cambridge University Press, 1992.

INDEX